MAKE IT YOURSELF!

COLORING & DOODLING

Paige V. Polinsky

Checkerboard
Library

An Imprint of Abdo Publishing
abdopublishing.com

abdopublishing.com

Published by Abdo Publishing, a division of ABDO, PO Box 398166, Minneapolis, Minnesota 55439. Copyright © 2018 by Abdo Consulting Group, Inc. International copyrights reserved in all countries. No part of this book may be reproduced in any form without written permission from the publisher. Checkerboard Library™ is a trademark and logo of Abdo Publishing.

Printed in the United States of America, North Mankato, Minnesota
062017
092017

THIS BOOK CONTAINS
RECYCLED MATERIALS

Design: Sarah DeYoung, Mighty Media, Inc.
Production: Mighty Media, Inc.
Editor: Liz Salzmann
Cover Photographs: Mighty Media, Inc.
Interior Photographs: iStockphoto; Mighty Media, Inc.; Shutterstock

The following manufacturers/names appearing in this book are trademarks: Behr Premium Plus®, Craft Smart®, Crayola®, Delta Creative™ Ceramcoat®, Elmer's®, Krylon®, Sharpie®, 3M™, Walgreens®

Publisher's Cataloging-in-Publication Data
Names: Polinsky, Paige V., author.
Title: Make it yourself! coloring & doodling / by Paige V. Polinsky.
Other titles: Make it yourself! coloring and doodling | Coloring and doodling
Description: Minneapolis, MN : Abdo Publishing, 2018. | Series: Cool makerspace | Includes bibliographical references and index.
Identifiers: LCCN 2016963037 | ISBN 9781532110689 (lib. bdg.) | ISBN 9781680788532 (ebook)
Subjects: LCSH: Makerspaces--Juvenile literature. | Handicraft--Juvenile literature.
Classification: DDC 680--dc23
LC record available at http://lccn.loc.gov/2016963037

TO ADULT HELPERS

This is your chance to assist a new maker! As children learn to use makerspaces, they develop new skills, gain confidence, and make cool things. These activities are designed to help children create projects in makerspaces. Children may need more assistance for some activities than others. Be there to offer guidance when they need it. Encourage them to do as much as they can on their own. Be a cheerleader for their creativity.

Before getting started, remember to lay down ground rules for using tools and supplies and for cleaning up. There should always be adult supervision when using a hot tool.

SAFETY SYMBOL

Some projects in this book require the use of hot tools. That means you'll need some adult help for these projects. Determine whether you'll need help on a project by looking for this safety symbol.

HOT!
This project requires the use of a hot tool.

CONTENTS

What's a
MAKERSPACE?

Imagine a place busy with people sketching, coloring, and doodling. Wide-open spaces invite you to plan, design, draw, and color. Colored pencils, crayons, markers, and other supplies surround you. Every material you can dream of is at your fingertips!

This is a makerspace. It is a place where people come together to create all kinds of cool stuff. Makers share sparks of creativity. They love to learn something new. They work together to design and create wonderful coloring and doodling projects. Are you ready to become a maker?

FUN WITH COLORING & DOODLING

The materials in a makerspace can lead to great ideas. Get inspired by the materials around you! Some projects can be shaped by the coloring and doodling supplies you have handy. Other projects will call for specific materials.

If your makerspace doesn't have something a project calls for, don't worry. Get creative! Remember, makers are problem-solvers. So, find another supply to substitute for the missing one. You'll be creating cool coloring projects and darling doodles in no time!

COLORING & DOODLING TIPS

Sharing is an important aspect of a makerspace. Makers share workspace, materials, and ideas. Being surrounded by other makers is great for creativity. But it also means a lot of projects may be happening at once. Here are some tips for successful makerspace projects.

HAVE A PLAN

Read through a project before beginning. Research any terms you may not know. Make sure you have everything you need for the project.

ASK FOR PERMISSION

Get **permission** from an adult to use the space, tools, and supplies.

BE RESPECTFUL

Before taking a tool or material, make sure another maker isn't using it.

KEEP YOUR SPACE CLEAN

Coloring and doodling projects can be messy. Keep crayons, pencils, and markers in containers so they don't roll around. Wear old clothes or an apron that you're allowed to get stained.

EXPECT MISTAKES & BE CREATIVE!

Being a maker isn't about creating something perfect. Have fun as you work!

SUPPLIES

Here are some of the materials and tools you'll need to do the projects in this book.

acrylic paint

acrylic sealer

card stock

clear dry-erase spray paint

colored pencils

cotton balls

double-sided tape

dry-erase marker

flat white latex paint

foam paintbrushes

glue stick

kraft paper

old CDs or DVDs

painter's tape

permanent
markers

ribbon

rocks

rubbing alcohol

toothpick

whiteboard
eraser

wooden dowels

wrapping
paper

COLORING & DOODLING TECHNIQUE

Try the Zentangle Method. A Zentangle is a drawing using repetitive patterns.

- Use a square sheet of white paper.

- Draw an outline lightly in pencil. It can be an object or a **random** shape. This will be the border of your design.

- Draw a curved line inside the border that divides the shape into sections. This is called the string.

- Start drawing a pattern along the string. This is called a tangle. Use black pen. Create a different tangle for each section.

DOODLE ROCKS

Turn plain old rocks into works of art!

10

1. Wash the rocks. Dry them completely.

2. Use a permanent marker to create patterns on the rocks.

3. Cover your work surface with newspaper. Brush a coat of acrylic sealer over the designs. Let the sealer dry.

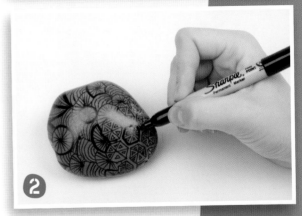

 **TIP** Try using colored markers to create colorful doodle rocks!

DOODLE
SHOES

Show off your style with these doodle-covered shoes!

WHAT YOU NEED

light-colored canvas shoes

ultra fine point permanent markers

fine point permanent markers

1. Draw a pattern on the shoes with an ultra fine point black marker. Cover both shoes completely. Let the ink dry.

2. Color your doodles with colored markers.

3. Don't forget to color the laces too! Use a thicker marker for a smoother look.

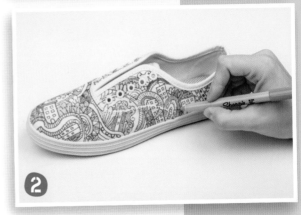

TIP When drawing the pattern, press lightly and move the marker quickly. If you press it too long in one spot, the **canvas** will **absorb** more ink. This can cause splotches.

ZANY DOODLE PORTRAIT

Transform friends and family
members with a little doodle magic!

WHAT YOU NEED

photograph of person

scissors

glue stick

card stock

pens

markers

colored pencils

1. Find or print a photograph of someone. It could be you, someone you know, or your favorite celebrity. Cut the image of the person out.

2. Glue the photo to a sheet of card stock.

3. Let the transformation begin! Draw a background scene or pattern around the person.

4. Color in the designs. Add a decorative border.

DISC SCRATCH ART MOBILE

Give old discs a new purpose with this colorful mobile.

WHAT YOU NEED

newspaper • old CDs or DVDs

acrylic paint • foam paintbrush

toothpick • ribbon • scissors

ruler • wooden dowel

1. Cover your work surface with newspaper. Paint the shiny side of each disc. Let the paint dry.

2. Use the toothpick to scratch designs and patterns into the paint. This reveals the shiny surface beneath.

3. Cut a piece of ribbon about 20 inches (50 cm) long. Tie the ends together.

4. Push the knot through a disc from back to front. Pull the knot through the loop of ribbon behind the disc.

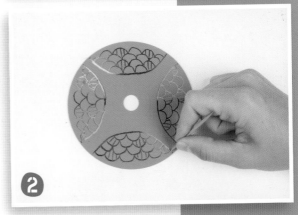

5. Repeat steps 3 and 4 to tie ribbons around the other discs. Try making them slightly different lengths.

6. Hang the discs on the dowel. Hang the dowel in front of a window. Watch how your art catches and reflects light!

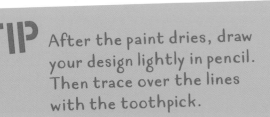

TIP After the paint dries, draw your design lightly in pencil. Then trace over the lines with the toothpick.

17

MUG ART

Sip your drinks in style!
Doodle on, bake, and cool
your own magnificent mug.

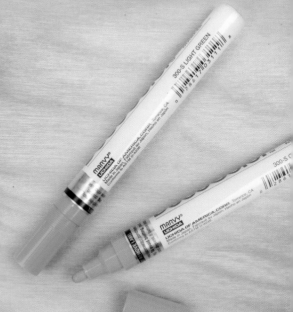

WHAT YOU NEED

plain white coffee mug
(porcelain works best)

rubbing alcohol • cotton balls

pencil • paper

paint pens • oven

18

1. Wipe the mug with rubbing alcohol and cotton balls. Let it dry.

2. Sketch your design in pencil on a sheet of paper. Draw a picture of something you like. Or create an **abstract** design. Write your name or an inspiring quote. Your mug can be whatever you want it to be!

3. Draw your sketched design on the mug with a black paint pen.

4. Use colored paint pens to add color to the design. Let the paint dry for 24 hours.

5. Place the mug in the oven. Turn the oven to 450 degrees Fahrenheit (232°C). After the oven reaches the set temperature, bake the mug for 45 minutes. Then turn off the oven, but leave the mug inside to cool.

6. Now your mug is ready to use! Hand wash it between uses. This will help keep the color from fading.

 TIP Make a mistake? That's okay! Just wipe the paint off with rubbing alcohol.

ANIMAL ANGLE ART

Use simple lines and angles to draw your favorite critter!

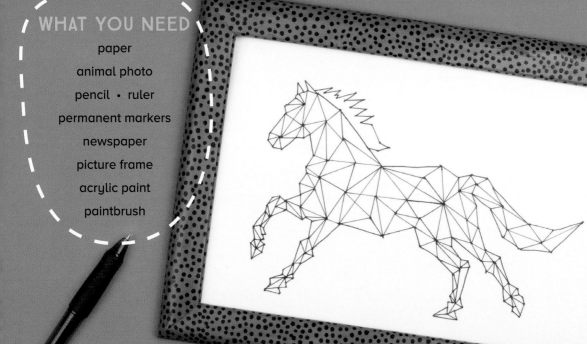

1. Place a sheet of paper over the animal photo. Trace the animal's outline with pencil. But only use straight lines. No curves!

2. Make small dots inside the outline. Then start creating angles! Connect the dots to different points on the outline and to one another. Use a ruler to keep the lines straight.

3. When you are happy with your angles, trace over the lines and the outline with permanent markers.

4. Cover your work surface with newspaper. Paint and decorate the picture frame. When it's dry, put your angle art in the frame.

DOODLE-POCKET BOOK COVER

Scribble on-the-go inspirations on this paper book cover. Slip doodle scraps into the pocket for safekeeping!

WHAT YOU NEED

book

wrapping paper

ruler

pencil

scissors

kraft paper

permanent markers

double-sided tape

1. Open the book and lay it flat on top of the wrapping paper. Line the bottom of the book up with the bottom edge of the paper.

2. Make several marks 2 inches (5 cm) up from the top of the book. Make several marks 2 inches (5 cm) out from each side of the book.

3. Set the book aside. Connect the marks to create a rectangle. Cut out the rectangle.

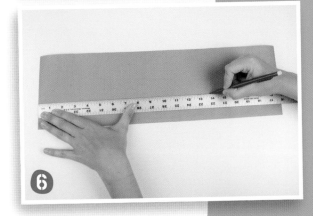

4. Fold the top of the wrapping-paper rectangle down 2 inches (5 cm).

5. Cut a piece of kraft paper the same width as the wrapping paper. The height should be half the height of the book plus 2 inches (5 cm). This will be the doodle pocket.

6. Draw a line 2 inches (5 cm) up from the bottom edge of the kraft paper.

7. Cover the area above the line with doodles.

Continued on the next page.

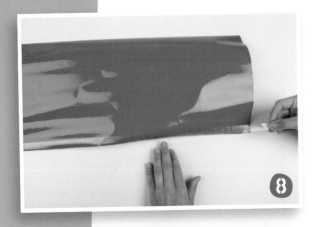

8 Turn the wrapping paper face up. Put double-sided tape along the bottom edge. Also put tape halfway up on each side. Make sure it is the same height as the pocket.

9 Press the kraft paper to the tape. Line the bottom of the doodle up with the bottom edge of the wrapping paper.

10 Turn the paper over. Fold the kraft paper up 2 inches (5 cm).

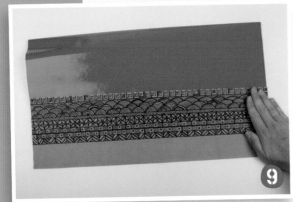

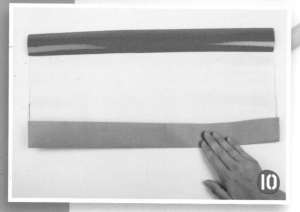

11. Fold each side in 2 inches (5 cm).

12. Place the open book in the center of the book cover.

13. Slip the front and back ends of the book into the cover.

14. Store notes and more doodles in the pocket.

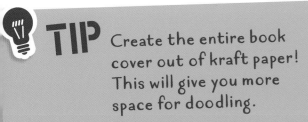

TIP Create the entire book cover out of kraft paper! This will give you more space for doodling.

DOODLE TABLE

Take your doodling skills to the next level with this reusable coloring table!

WHAT YOU NEED

small coffee table • newspaper

painter's tape • flat white latex paint

paintbrush • pencil • ruler

permanent marker

clear dry-erase spray paint

dry-erase markers • whiteboard eraser

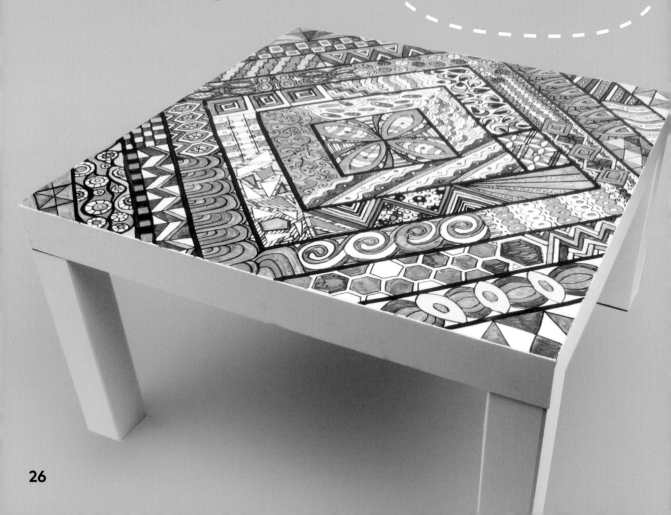

1. If the table's legs are removable, take them off. Set the legs aside.

2. Cover your work surface with newspaper. Put painter's tape around the sides of the tabletop.

3. Paint the tabletop with flat white latex paint. Let the paint dry. Add a second coat of paint. Let it dry.

4. Use a pencil and ruler to divide the tabletop into sections.

Continued on the next page.

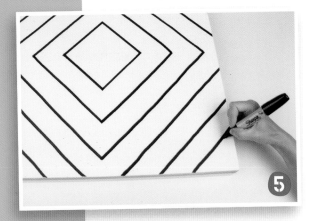

5 Trace over the section lines with permanent marker.

6. Draw patterns on the tabletop in pencil. Create a different design in each section. Continue adding doodles until the tabletop is filled.

7 Trace over the doodle lines with permanent marker.

8. Have an adult help spray the tabletop with clear dry-erase paint. Let it dry.

9. Put the legs back on the table if you removed them in step 1.

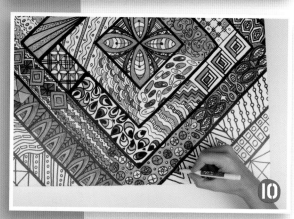

10 Color the doodle with dry-erase markers. When the pattern is filled, wipe clean and start again!

BRIGHT IDEA!

You can find coloring and doodling supplies **online**, at craft stores, and at office supply stores. You can also find them at **thrift stores** and **garage sales**.

Use bins to keep your supplies organized. Sort markers, crayons, and pencils by type and color instead of keeping them in their original boxes. Then when you're coloring and doodling, you can easily find what you need.

PLAN A MAKER EVENT!

Being a maker is not just about the finished product. It is about communication, **collaboration**, and creativity. Do you have a project you'd like to make with the support of a group? Then make a plan and set it in action!

SECURE A SPACE

Think of places that would work well for a makerspace. This could be a library, school classroom, or space in a community center. Then, talk to adults in charge of the space. Describe your project. Tell them how you would use the space and keep it organized and clean.

INVITE MAKERS

Once you have a space, it is time to spread the word! Work with adults in charge of the space to determine how to do this. You could make an e-invitation, create flyers about your maker event, or have family and friends tell others.

MATERIALS & TOOLS

Materials and tools cost money. How will you supply these things? **Brainstorm** ways to raise money for your makerspace. You could plan a fund-raiser to buy needed items. You could also ask makers to bring their own supplies.

GLOSSARY

absorb — to soak up or take in.

abstract — in art, expressing ideas or emotions without attempting to create a realistic picture.

brainstorm — to come up with a solution by having all members of a group share ideas.

canvas — a firm, closely woven cloth usually made of linen, hemp, or cotton. It is used to make clothing, tents, and sails.

collaboration — the act of working with another person or group in order to do something or reach a goal.

garage sale — a sale that takes place in someone's yard or garage.

online — connected to the Internet.

permission — when a person in charge says it's okay to do something.

random — without any order, purpose, or method.

thrift store — a store that sells used items, especially one that is run by a charity.

WEBSITES

To learn more about Cool Makerspace, visit **abdobooklinks.com**. These links are routinely monitored and updated to provide the most current information available.

INDEX